HOW TO BE LUCKY

by

WENDY GRANT

Illustrations by Tony Thornhill

First published in the United Kingdom in 1994 by
Eastbrook Publishing, Trull, Taunton, Somerset, England. TA3 7LQ.

Copyright © Wendy Grant 1994
ISBN 0 9518812 3 X

All rights reserved. No part of this publication may be reproduced, stored in a retrieval system, or transmitted, in any form or by any means, without the prior permission of the publisher.

Printed in Great Britain by
Redwood Books, Trowbridge, Wiltshire.

British Cataloguing-in-Publication Data. A catalogue record for this book is available from the British Library.

OTHER BOOKS BY WENDY GRANT

Available by post from Eastbrook Publishing, Trull, Taunton, Somerset, TA3 7LQ. Tel: 0823 321233

Are You In Control? - a step by step book for those who want to be in control of their own lives. £4.85

Dare! - a positive guide to being yourself. £5.50

Going Back - an extraordinary true story to warm your heart. £5.95

For Real - a mystery thriller, created by Sadie Thornhill, written by Wendy Grant. £6.50

Available by post from Mendip Publishing, Castle Cary Press, Yeovil.

Secrets - a carefully designed story to help children differentiate between good and bad secrets. One of the most important books you will ever read with your child - a *must* for every caring parent. £3.50

Sam's Secret - the first in a series of six complete stories designed to help children resolve emotional and behavioural problems. £3.50

Note: Please add £1.00 towards postage and packing.

- **How to get what you want**

- **How to win**

- **How to be financially successful**

- **How to be lucky in love**

- **How to dream solutions**

- **How to manage materialistic gain**

- **How to develop a new awareness**

HOW TO BE LUCKY

Are some people really born lucky? Is it luck that finds certain people in the right place at the right time? How is that some people win prizes so frequently while others never win anything?

What is luck and does it really exist? Or is it just a convenient word to express that which we do not understand?

Luck certainly allows us to opt out, or to blame something else for things we believe are outside our control.

The dictionary describes luck as: things that appear to come by chance; one's fate or lot; to profit or gain; the fortuitous happening of fortunate - or adverse events; afflicted by a misfortune.

It's just my bad luck! He always seems so lucky! How often have you made these or similar statements? It is as if luck were something quite separate from ourselves, that we have no control over what happens on the 'luck scene'.

However, I am now convinced, after much research and experimentation, that this is not so. In the following pages I set out, not only to prove that you *do* have an active part to play in luck, but also to show how *you* can become lucky.

CONTENTS

BECOMING AWARE - TAKING CONTROL
   Before you begin 13
   Investigating Luck 13
   Taking a Positive Look at Your Childhood 15
   Assessing Your Own Skills 17
   Expectation 20
   Cause and Effect 21
   In The Right Place at The Right Time 23
   Beyond Our Senses 25
   Stress 26

HOW TO GET WHAT YOU WANT
   Gambling 30
   Programming 36
   Programming with the Moon Phases 38

GOOD HEALTH
   Where Does It All Start? 40
   Your Health in Your Hands 40
   Accidents 43

LUCKY IN LOVE
   This Thing Called Love 45
   The Way You Are 46
   How a Relationship Can Work 47
   A Positive Viewpoint 48
   How a Viewpoint Changes our Perception 49
   When Love is Not Returned 50
   Sex 51

CONTENTS

SUPERSTITIONS AND LUCKY NUMBERS
Fear 54
Dealing with Fear 54
Superstitions 56
Lucky Mascots and Lucky Charms 58
Body Language 59
Getting Closer To Reality 60
Numbers - Lucky or Unlucky? 61

USING YOUR DREAMS
What Dreams Tell Us 63
Creative Dreaming 64
Dream Symbols 66
The Words We Use 66
Transporting a Thought 67

MANAGEMENT OF SUCCESS
How Things Go Wrong 71
Humility 72
Learning from Children 74
The Underlying Need to Succeed 75
The Unconscious Choice 75
Spirituality and Conscious Awareness 76
Summary 77
Finally 77

BECOMING AWARE - TAKING CONTROL

Before You Begin

Make a list of all those things you believe are dependent on luck. Do you believe that winning the pools, being born into a well-off family, or missing a bus that goes on to crash further down the road are all due to luck? Then put them on your list.

If you think that certain people are lucky, identify those areas in which you think they are lucky and detail lucky occurrences or attributes. Do certain numbers seem lucky or unlucky for you? Are there certain periods in your own life which have seemed to be unlucky?

When you have completed your list, put it on one side and carry on reading.

Investigating Luck

It was about 10.15 one night, about thirty years ago, when I realised that luck - good or bad - was not simply something that happened to you. At that time I had three children under the age of four, and although it was quite late, I was standing at the ironing board chatting to a young friend while ironing the children's clothes.

Suddenly she looked up at me and said, "You are lucky!"

I stared at her. It was the very last thing I had been thinking. "What makes you say that?" I asked.

"Well . . . . to have three beautiful healthy children, a wonderful husband, and this house."

"That's not luck," I responded. "That's the result of sheer hard work eighteen hours a day."

She didn't understand. I tried to explain, but she was then only sixteen and had to learn about life for herself.

That conversation did, however, make me stop and think very carefully about what had made me reply in that way. The house, which was situated close to the beach, was large and a real pain to keep clean, and expensive to maintain. We had bought it so that my husband's parents could be looked after by us. They were elderly and had reached the point where they needed someone to be on call most of the time. Our offering them a home had resulted, quite unexpectedly, in them giving us the deposit to put down on the house.

So was I lucky? Two elderly disabled people and three small children to care for may not be everyone's idea of being lucky. My *good luck,* as noted by my young friend, was actually due to the way she viewed what I had.

As to the wonderful, caring husband - well, I had *chosen* him, thanks partly, I believed, to the very good example of a partnership demonstrated to me by my own parents. In addition, keeping a husband happy meant having time for him at the end of a long exhausting day, and making the effort to be the partner and lover he desired, when often all I wanted to do was fall asleep. As to the healthy children - was that luck, or did my previous life style play a part? I had never smoked, didn't care for alcohol, and taught ballroom dancing part-time which kept me fit and agile throughout my pregnancies.

I began to think that we may have considerable control over luck - in at least some areas of our lives.

Since that night, I have had more than thirty years to observe so-called *luck* in action, and I am now convinced that we can *make* things happen. *We **do** have an influence.*

It is not just your viewpoint that enables you to see things positively and to grasp opportunities when they arise, by using your mind and visualisation, you can help to create all the good fortune you wish.

Taking a Positive Look at Your Childhood

Many people believe that the family and environment into which we are born is the luck of the draw - others believe that we, as a spiritual entity, choose our physical role as part of a growth and awareness experience.

Whatever you may believe, some children certainly appear to be born 'disadvantaged'. This means that in some way or ways, they have less than others. This can be in the parents they have and/or the environment for development and growth in which they find themselves.

It may be that you were born with a physical disability; you may have been placed in a 'home' and never experienced a caring family; you may have parents who are drug addicts. Disadvantaged? If you read the histories of successful people you will often find that it was *because* of their very disability that they achieved so much. Their adversity or disadvantage actually helped them or motivated them to achieve.

Many successful people have come from violent or non-loving families. Others were cast out and had to survive on their own from an incredibly early age. We know that Stalin had a withered arm, and that President Roosevelt of America was bound to a wheelchair - their disadvantages didn't prevent *them* from achieving.

Kriss Akabusi is a modern example of a youth who struggled to survive despite numerous disadvantages. At the age of three he was taken from his English home to Nigeria where he experienced poverty, physical beatings, and lost any real communication with his father. A year later he was returned to England and placed in a succession of foster homes. When he was eight his parents split up and the civil war in Nigeria brought an end to all financial support and communication. Despite all this, Kriss went on to become European, Commonwealth and World champion, he gained three Olympic medals and an MBE for services to sport.

So what makes such people succeed? We can hardly say they were lucky. They did, however, take their adversities and turn them into challenges.

While some use their hard-luck stories as a reason for not achieving, others use their handicaps as a spur to better things.

Once I asked my father, who came from one of the poorer parts of Birmingham, why he never used bad language. As an engineer working on the shop-floor he must have heard swearing and foul language daily. "I've worked hard to give us a better standard of living than I had as a child," he told me. "If you choose to use bad language you are putting yourself back in the gutter." Then he gave me one of his little smiles. "It's up to you," he said. "You always have a choice."

He had taken his childhood and used it as an incentive to work towards achieving a better life.

We cannot go back and change our childhood, parents, or experiences at school, but we can see them as extremely beneficial if we use them to our ultimate advantage.

I recently read that as parents we need to fail in order that our children may learn from such experiences. It is a novel way of looking at life, and a good one for pulling us up short from playing the 'blame game'.

When we stop using blame as an excuse, we can begin to take responsibility for our own actions and responses instead of feeling helpless. If you have ever met a child who has always had everything, you will realise why parents need sometimes to fail in some areas - it is the only way the child can learn about life and not end up as a spoilt, obnoxious brat.

Exercise One

1. Write down all your childhood experiences that you have been seeing (and perhaps using) in a negative way. No one else is going to read it, so be honest. If you feel that your father neglected you, or your mother expected too much from you, write it down. If you had a teacher who scared the wits out of

you so that you could never learn maths, make a note of it. And if you lived five floors up in an apartment block and never had the opportunity to play in open spaces, put it on your list. Include all those things over which you really did have very little control (because you were then young and dependent).

2. Now consider how you could turn your negative responses to some of those experiences into positive responses or actions. As soon as you do this you take control and you are no longer a victim. Help this along by using your visual ability - get your imagination working for you. If maths is a problem because of a certain teacher you had, realise that you are free now to go back and attend a maths course if that's what you want to do. Perhaps it is sufficient to simply realise that you are not stupid or 'thick' but that the way in which you were taught was wrong. If you had a harsh, uncaring father, see how you can use that experience to love more, to give to *your* child the time and understanding that was lacking in your own childhood. Certainly from such experiences you will learn to value your time with your child in a truly wonderful way. Where you were constantly being told by a parent that you were useless and stupid, you are now old enough to realise that it was the parent who had the problem - use it as a spur to go on and prove how capable you really are - you don't *have* to go on believing what others said. Always remember that ***you have a choice.***

Right, so you have taken control. From this moment onwards start using this new awareness to see how you can take experiences from your past and put them to positive use.

Assessing Your Own Skills

Let us look now at your education which began in your childhood and hopefully will continue throughout your life. Whether you had an expensive private education, an average state one, or virtually none at all, you will certainly have learned *something*. Just living is a learning experience.

How has your learning helped you? What sort of a person have you become? Most of us spend too much time concerning ourselves with how we look, and not nearly enough working with *who* we are.

Are you practical? Artistic? Good at communicating? Do you have a retentive memory? Are you creative in some areas of your life? Have you developed the skills to listen, to organise, or to manage a budget efficiently? How have you been using your natural talents? Have you been helping yourself to luck by cashing in on what you do naturally well?

Are you practical? Artistic? Good at communicating?

Do you believe that you have been *lucky* in getting the job you want?

I received a phone call the other day from a lady who had made over three hundred job applications and failed to get one interview. "I'm just plain unlucky," she informed me. However, as she continued to talk, I realised that her real problem lay in her total lack of belief in herself. She *expected* to be rejected.

If you made a hundred job applications without getting any results, wouldn't you try to do *something* different?

We have all learned how to stay alive - but are you doing it in the best way possible for you? Does your life give you a sense of fulfilment and joy? Are you making things happen or waiting for some good luck to come your way?

Sometimes feeling helpless gives us the excuse to stay where we are; change requires courage, strength and determination. However fearsome change may appear, when you look at where you are right now, probably almost anything is better than doing nothing.

Kriss Akabusi, talking to a group of youngsters in Ulster, told them that once you achieve in one thing, you know you can achieve anything you want. This applies to us all.

Pause here for a few minutes and ask yourself, *what do I want*? And then, *why do I want it*? Start to get to know yourself. Often, when we put thoughts into words, we can see a clear plan of action begin to emerge.

A True Story

When the youngest son of a friend was about fourteen years of age, she asked him one day to pop into the new butcher's shop at the end of the road and buy some meat. He could have said he was doing something else, or didn't have time, or moaned until she weakened and went herself - but he left with a cheerful, '*Bye*', and she returned to her chores.

Her son returned half an hour later to tell her that he had been offered a Saturday job by the butcher.

"What made him ask you?" she enquired, surprised.

"I don't know. I just walked in at the right moment I suppose," he replied.

But a dozen boys had probably been in the shop since it had opened, so why offer him the job?

When she got to know the butcher she asked him.

"It was the way he walked in," he explained. "I took an instant liking to him and he joked and made us smile."

If I believed in it, I would say that good luck has continued to follow him around, but I know it is more than that. That invisible *something* which appears to make some people so lucky, is available to us all.

Have you noticed the way everything seems to go right for some people? Folks think it happens by magic, they fail to see that the *lucky* person had choices and instinctively chose the best ones available to him or her.

Expectation

Expectation is one of the most powerful forces in our lives, and yet few use it. Have you ever tried to go though one of those doors where an automatic spring loaded device causes the door to close on you when you are halfway through with your arms full of shopping? Next time, picture someone holding the door open for you - I guarantee it will work.

Expecting people to like us means that we send out the right signals. If you put up your defences, coat yourself in invisible prickles, look for every sign that a person is criticising you or having a laugh at you, then you will find it hard indeed to make friends.

Expecting the job interview to go well does have an effect as you unconsciously send out the right signals. Expecting to do well in exams means that you unconsciously programme yourself to put in the effort and to view study positively. It *is* difficult to study for long hours if you are expecting to fail.

When we picture something, we send out an invisible message. Thought is energy that takes form as vibration - and people are affected by vibration. Ultrasonic sound (which is vibration) is now used medically to assist in healing. *It has an effect.*

Cause and Effect

The more fully we understand *cause and effect*, the more we can make it work for us.

If you are a driver, the next time you go into town, picture a parking space and drive directly to it. I know many people who do this and return to my classes to tell me with a big grin, *"It really does work."*

This doesn't happen by magic, luck or coincidence. In a wonderful way that we don't yet understand, we are becoming aware of a situation by other than the normal route of our five senses.

Note: I just have to add this experience, though this manuscript is now completed. I drove into town an hour ago and as I approached the car park I realised I had no change. A woman driving out opened her window and passed me her ticket. "There's an hour left on this, can you use it?" she asked. Was it coincidence, luck, or did we telepathically communicate?

Have you ever thought of someone, perhaps an old friend or acquaintance whom you haven't seen or heard from for ages, and then they phone, or a letter from them drops through the letter box? To your surprise, 'out of the blue', they make contact.

Next time it happens, don't brush it aside as coincidence - *notice it!* You will begin to see just how often this kind of thing happens. Your thoughts don't stay inside your head, there is no reason why they should, for they are not made of flesh, blood or bones, but tiny electro-magnetic impulses - they are part of the 'whole' that makes up our universe.

Animals have always known it - for this we have a name, we call it instinct; it's a wonderful word to describe what we don't understand. A tiny bird doesn't fly 4,000 miles hoping by coincidence or luck to arrive at a certain piece of land where it may safely spend the winter. We wouldn't think of calling the bird *lucky* that it *happened* to land in the right place at the right time.

But when *we* travel only a few miles and manage to arrive safely at our destination without using a map, I wouldn't mind betting that we would describe ourselves as lucky.

Ah! But that's different, you may protest. Hold on a minute! Of course, by using our training and consciously applying logic and gained information we can get around - most of us operate this way most of the time. What I am saying is that there is *another* way of living in our environment that enables us to operate outside, or beyond, the normal senses of sight, sound, touch, smell and taste - it is one which we would do well to heed and to develop.

Edgar Cayce (now deceased) is known as one of the world's greatest psychics. He was able to interpret his own, and other's dreams, so accurately that people became rich by following the knowledge he gained by accessing this other part of self. He dreamed of mines and oil wells, and when to buy and sell on the stock market; he taught people to interpret their own dreams and to take control of their own lives. Many became millionaires by following his guidance.

He also warned that those who sought fame or power over others, or as compensation for their own failures or guilt, would not benefit from their financial success. He saw nothing wrong with having materialistic possessions - so long as they didn't become the focal point or ultimate aim of that person.

He became a deeply spiritual man, knowing that his ability to step outside the normal senses was something he had to share with others. It changed his life and now helps to open doors for those of us who are prepared to make the effort and take the time to reach a deeper, richer, understanding of our place in the universe.

Using logic can work within a system - at least some of the time. But when we go beyond thought, we access another source: we can **KNOW** with a knowledge that has nothing to do with conscious thought.

In The Right Place at The Right Time

Some people account for their good fortune by reasoning that they were in the right place at the right time. But why were they there? When we ask questions like this we begin to get the right answers.

Obviously, conscious logical progression of thought enables us to be in a certain location when it is *most likely* we will benefit from being there. It is no good being on holiday in the Caribbean if you want to be elected as a local government councillor when the voting is going on. There are, however, other ways that go beyond logic that can not only benefit us, but can even save our lives.

A True Story Demonstrating Cause and Effect

During World War Two I lived with my parents outside the city of Birmingham. Often we were awakened by sirens warning us to take cover as enemy planes were in the vicinity. If search lights prevented them from dropping bombs over the industrial areas, the pilots would off-load their bombs before making a rapid retreat. Our village was directly beneath their air route.

As the husbands of our neighbours on either side of us were away, and the wives had small children, they would all assemble in our house in response to the air raid warning. Then, when it was considered safe to make a run for it, we would all dash out of doors, up the road, and into the cellars beneath my grandfather's house.

On one such night we were all crammed into the hall of our house waiting to make a run for it when my mother's voice called out: "Wait! Everyone get under the stairs."

We squashed ourselves into an even smaller space in the walk-in cupboard once used as a larder. It was hot and stuffy and one of the babies smelled of sick. I recall longing to run outside into the fresh air.

Suddenly there was a tremendous noise. The house trembled and shook and someone screamed aloud.

Outside the front gate a bomb had landed and exploded ripping the water mains apart. If we hadn't listened to my mother it would have killed all of us.

What had made her stop us from going out at that precise moment? How could she have *known?*

The wardens who came to investigate said how lucky we were to be alive. But it wasn't luck. It had been mother, listening to her 'inner self' who had saved us from destruction.

A Very Different Example of Cause and Effect

Wilf wanted to change his job and run a business of his own. He was very interested in motorcycles and hated the repetitive job he had in a shoe factory. To him the idea of mending and working with motorbikes was the nearest he would ever get to a perfect existence. But he had no capital, and with three children to support his idea seemed little more than a dream.

In his spare time he helped an elderly neighbour with his allotment as the old man was too stiff to do his own digging. One day Wilf mentioned motorbikes to the man. He responded enthusiastically. He used to have a Norton he told Wilf; then he'd bought an old Rudge. He began to reminisce and Wilf listened with respect. He realised that beneath that battered hat was a wealth of knowledge that would be lost to future generations.

A few weeks later the old man asked Wilf if he would like to see something - he wouldn't say more, he wanted it to be a surprise. Wilf went with him to a lockup garage in another part of town. When the old man opened the doors Wilf could not believe his eyes. Six wonderful old bikes were stored inside. "I couldn't bear to let them go," he told Wilf. "I don't suppose they are worth anything now - but I thought you might like to have a look."

From that moment the two of them set to work rebuilding the bikes. It took years. The old neighbour died and left the bikes to Wilf in his will. Wilf could not believe his 'good luck'. It was another five years before he could afford to give up his factory job and open his bike museum. During that time people got to hear about Wilf, old bikes of every make were being donated to 'his dream'. Men, like his old neighbour, who no longer had the motivation or ability to rebuild their bikes themselves, were only too happy to think Wilf could make them look as good as new.

This is where we so often mistake 'cause and effect' for luck. Wilf didn't set out to gain from helping the old man, and it is often such an act of selflessness that initiates the success or achievement which we put down to luck.

Beyond Our Senses

The more we are in tune with ourselves and our universe, the more we will sense the inner, intuitive awareness that is a vital part of every living creature. It is there in plants - they know when to fold their leaves or petals before a storm; moles know when to move to higher ground before the floods; birds know when to migrate early before the onset of a hard winter.

The problem is that we have become so dependent on our physical senses that we have moved further and further away from being aware of our true place in the universe; we deny that anything we can't experience through our normal five senses exists. And yet things are happening all the time to remind us - we just don't pay attention.

Western civilisation, more than any other, is guilty of this, and our quality of life is the poorer for it.

It is time now to begin training yourself to this greater awareness if you ever want 'to be lucky'. Awareness and choice is what luck is all about - they are available to anyone.

Notes:
1. Remember that expectation is a powerful force - encompass this belief absolutely. Practise thinking positively. *Your thoughts will always have an effect.* Whenever you catch yourself thinking negatively, STOP, and turn it around. If you just miss the bus, see it as a wonderful opportunity to take exercise and

walk home, or use the time to observe the world around you, or memorise something that would be useful to you in the future.

2. Know that all the good things that you see happening to others can also happen to you. Begin to see yourself achieving and receiving - do this as if it were a reality and not in a wishful dreamy way.

3. Believe you deserve good things to happen - you have as much right to good fortune as any other person.

4. When you have a 'gut feeling', when you feel intuitively that something is right or wrong, go along with it - it is usually far more accurate than all your logical calculations.

All this should soon become second nature to you if you really practise it. By this I mean that you integrate it naturally into your everyday life. You will, however, find it quite hard to achieve if you are stressed - so deal with any stress that is getting in the way.

Stress

To set yourself free to operate at this new level of awareness you need to get rid of negative responses to stress. Most of stress is caused by the way we view things; changing your viewpoint will help to reduce stress in many areas of your life. If you can't change something or avoid it, the best thing to do is change the way you view it.

I have often found that turning a stressful situation into a cartoon inside my head can work wonders. And with many situations that used to annoy, irritate or upset me, I now find it sufficient to say to myself, *it's only a little thing.*

Have you ever cut your finger and found yourself moaning about how sore it is or how inconvenient? Yet all the time the rest of your body was completely well and without pain or discomfort - *and you didn't even notice it!*

Someone in a restaurant may take the last available table which you thought was yours - compared with all the terrible things that can happen in life it is, after all, *only a little thing.* The situation can also offer you the chance to try somewhere new that becomes a future favourite when you dine out. Or you could return home fed up and disillusioned blaming your bad luck, saying something like, "This sort of thing always happens to me."

When someone close to you says something hurtful, or does something without consideration for your feelings, before getting upset, compare it with all the positive things that that person does. Usually you can then see that it was, after all, *only a little thing*.

For goodness sake, don't use up your precious energy being stressed when there are so many other wonderful things you could be doing with your mind and energy.

Remind yourself that, "It's only a little thing."

From now on, take fifteen minutes a day to do the following exercise:

Exercise Two - Relaxation

1. Make yourself physically comfortable in an armchair or on your bed. Breathe deeply for a few minutes and concentrate on the rhythm of your breathing.

2. Now close your eyes and notice how you feel as you let go and relax. Notice how each part of you feels, starting with your toes and feet and working up over your body. End back at your breathing. Where you find areas that are very tense and won't seem to relax - most likely your stomach muscles, shoulders or neck - tense this area even more for a few seconds and then let go and relax.

3. Visualise yourself in a place that spells total peace to you. This may be in your own bed; the bath; lying on a golden sandy beach; sitting on a river bank. Build the picture in your head as clearly as you can, adding the texture of things, the sounds, smells and taste where appropriate. Experience this as fully as you can.

4. Give this scene a special name, one you can recall instantly when you have the need to relax. Now open your eyes and think about something that causes in you a stressful response. This may be someone at work, being late and stuck in a traffic queue, a visit from your mother-in-law. As the stressful response to your thoughts begins to return, say your special word and let your mind return for a few seconds to your peaceful place. The feelings of calm *will* return.

Note: You can use this technique any time you are under stress. You are *choosing* a different response that puts you in control. (Further help with stress is available in my book "Are You In Control?")

So what has all this to do with luck? We miss out and often fail to notice many opportunities when we are stressed. Stress may also prevent us from tapping on to that special awareness where extraordinary things can and do happen.

Opening ourselves to other energies will enable us to experience enlightenment. Suddenly we see clearly. We understand.

HOW TO GET WHAT YOU WANT

Gambling

Have you ever known someone who always seems to be winning prizes or competitions? Do you know someone who comes up on the pools or premium bonds far more often than is dictated by chance?

"Now," you are going to say to me, "that can only be luck! You can't *make* that happen!"

WRONG! You can!

You don't believe me? Read on . . . .

Let us first look at people who gamble. Most of us have at least tried those machines with tantalising flashing lights found in almost every pub, road service area, club, or place of entertainment. Have you stood and watched someone empty the machine, and have you followed on a lucky run only to lose every single coin you put in?

Do you know that these machines are programmed to pay out around 80 to 85% of the takings? Computer softwear used in the machine is designed so that the pay out can be changed should it be found that competition is drawing players away. Although individual owners are not allowed to benefit directly from machines in clubs, similar controls are exercised. All gambling machines are carefully designed and controlled by computers - *nothing is actually left to chance*.

If you had the time and were capable of observing, recording and doing the necessary calculations, you could predict when a player was going to win. But it is far too complex so I wouldn't advise you to try - there are better ways of winning that we will come to in a minute.

The strange thing is the fact that although it is the owners, landlords or businesses that ultimately benefit from gambling, this does not seem to matter to the gambler. Every player believes, for some strange intangible reason, that luck can be his or hers for the time they are playing. Surely, no one plays to lose!

People have invented and tried just about every permutation, calculation and trick to beat the roulette wheel. The players must win some of the time - just enough to keep them coming back. Those who run casinoes are extremely clever business people; an occasional big win looks good and gives a player hope that next time it could be his/her turn to be lucky. A recent survey showed that even a small computer hidden in the toe of a shoe was used by some players to work out the odds - it was illegal, of course. The verdict was that we would be better off putting our money into a building society.

Folks are very good at deluding themselves, they do this by recalling the times they won, and often precisely how much. They rarely calculate how much they lose. They don't mind losing sometimes, they will tell you, it's good entertainment, a nice day or evening out. Who are they kidding? They go to win!

Bingo has become an increasingly popular area of gambling for the housewife. It is convenient, not too expensive, and can be played in the afternoons if you can't get out at night. Not many end the year with more than they started with, but there is the element of excitement, and the rise in adrenaline that gives them a boost. They also enjoy the companionship and don't come away feeling *too* disappointed when they lose.

How about winning prizes offered daily in competitions? They come regularly through the letter box; they are in every national newspaper, magazine, children's comic; they are on cans and packets of everything from soap powder to soups.

A letter will arrive telling us how close we are to winning a car, a holiday abroad or a vast sum of money - we are often informed that our lucky numbers have already been selected for us, that we have only to return the card, form, or letter. Of course, if we buy their product we have the feeling our numbers are more likely to get put in the hat. You *know* it is all done because they want your money. They don't really have any intention of making you a present of anything without getting *something* out of it.

There are ways in which you *can* win. It has become a business in itself for some people; they rush out and purchase the necessary goods with the competition rules printed on the labels, or they pour over word games and puzzles in papers and magazines. If you follow these kinds of competitions closely, you begin to get a *feeling* for what the promoters want, or the kind of slogans that are used as a deciding factor.

There are even businesses set up where the operators will select the competitions for you and guarantee that you will win *some* of the prizes. The trouble is that most of us don't have the stamina to withstand the pressure of hours and hours of study that is required. But some do, and they will tell you it's not really down to luck, you just have to keep at it.

Card playing, we know, in certain games, is dependent to a great extent on the hand we are dealt. So why is it that some people seem to get the best hands? A good memory, a thorough knowledge of the game, body language, all play an important part. But do some players go beyond that? Do they have the right mental attitude to relax and *visualise* the right cards falling to them? Can they influence the game this way? And is it done naturally or have they somehow discovered 'the secret'?

I know that many people think gambling is wrong or even wicked. We must, however, remember that those who play cards *choose* to do so - no one makes them. An addicted gambler may feel that he or she has no choice, but *they do,* and can be helped to overcome the compulsion once they decide to seek help.

Life itself is very much a gamble; we play the hand we are dealt in life according to how we perceive life working for or against us. **What I am endeavouring to do is to help you take control.** The way in which you use your gains or treat others is your personal choice and part of your growth. (*More about this later.*)

What about greyhound racing? I can recall the time when I used to run boarding kennels and would often look after greyhounds for their owners. The owners only ever bet on a certainty. One thing was for sure, race a bitch just when she came into season and no male dog would pass her on the track. Of course you weren't *supposed* to race them when they 'broke down' (the term used for bitches in season), but before there was any physical evidence only the owner knew.

Studying form and taking a knowledgeable interest in horse racing, can make a difference to your chances. But most of us know very little about horses and bet on impulse - perhaps we like the horse's name, or the way he tosses his head.

And what of Edgar Cayce? How could his dreams have so successfully predicted success? He didn't use any of the systems the gambler uses, he trusted totally in his other resources, recognising that what went on when he was sleeping was more reliable than the frailty of the physical human body and its conscious senses. At a different level, he had the answers.

When we, by what seems to be luck, choose a winner, we are doing what Cayce did - tapping on to the Universal Consciousness that can travel backwards or forwards in time. Having a premonition is the same thing, and we all experience those from time to time.

As all modern scientists will tell you, time is only a concept of man, used as a measure in our space/time existence. *It doesn't really exist.*

If you find this hard to believe, read any modern scientific book. Using sophisticated telescopes, space travel and computers, they know how time changes, how it is distorted by gravitation, how it eventually folds back in on itself.

For you to benefit, it is enough to know that one can step outside time and have certain knowledge and experiences not available in the conventional way.

You have probably had the experience of buying someone a gift, a CD for example, and as you hand it over you get the response, "How on earth did you know? I've just bought a CD player!" *What made you buy it? How did you know?*

Stop and think of the last time something like that happened to you. Don't write it off as coincidence, see it as evidence that is part of the foundation of your new knowledge and belief - *you have control, you have choices, you have the ability to know and to see in a different way.*

Some people who successfully invest in the stock market will tell you that they just had 'this feeling' that it was the right time to invest or to withdraw. It was this same 'awareness' that warned Edgar Cayce of the stock market collapse in the States in 1929.

Stepping outside time can be done at will, as demonstrated by truly clairvoyant people. The results have been well documented many times. Despite the charlatans and those whose claims would discourage us, certain people demonstrate a knowledge of things or happenings that cannot possibly have been attained through any of the normal senses. These people are genuinely clairvoyant. In laboratory tests they score far higher than astrologists, palmists, or numerologists.

If you are not naturally gifted in this way, you can train yourself, but it is a hard discipline and takes years. However, a shorter route is available. I have tried and tested it, and for me, at least, it seems to work just as well, where what was once thought of as 'luck' is involved. I believe it can be used by anyone with the will to persevere. As you practice in this way and get results, your belief system will be strengthened until you can truly have all you wish for.

There are a few golden rules that I find it pays to follow:

a) Whatever you want, look at the intention behind your desire. If it is truly good and will harm no one, go ahead. Where there is any doubt, re-think what you are wanting.

You may want to change your job because you hate the boss. Here you need to work through your feelings not run away from them. Deal with the problem first, then by all means change your job if that is what you still desire and believe will improve your quality of life.

You want a lot of money - most of us want more than we have. But what is your intention? Do you want to spend it in a beneficial way, to provide a better quality of life for your family, a better education for the children? If you see it as a means of impressing people you had better re-think, it could lead to disillusionment.

Some years ago a national newspaper followed up six people who had won enormous sums of money on the football pools. All had lost the lot. They were very bitter, disappointed people. Those they had sought to help had let them down, others had taken without giving anything in return; possessions had not lead to happiness; investments had collapsed. They were aware that they had behaved foolishly. We all think we would do better, few of us, however, have the strength of character.

b) Be very precise in deciding what you do want. Ask yourself, *what do I really want*? If you want money, it doesn't have to be through winning the premium bonds, the pools or through betting on a race horse. An unexpected inheritance would fulfil your needs in the same way. If it is peace of mind that you want, there may be another way of attaining it that has nothing to do with money.

c) Think beyond the receiving. Can you cope with the results of getting what you want? Who else will it affect?

Be very precise in deciding what you want.

Programming

Using the moon phases. Having read about this many years ago, and after repeatedly hearing it discussed since by writers, cosmologists and psychic people, I decided to investigate.

We all know that the moon affects our planet and that the tides are controlled by the powerful pull of the moon. Whole masses of water covering the majority of the surface of our planet respond to the moon's phases.

As we are made up mostly of water, I reasoned that we might also expect to be influenced by the moon. (It was from here that the word *lunatic* originated). The only way to put this to the test was by using my own visual programming with the moon phases.

It is suggested that we use our visualisation as an outgoing force to get what we want at the time of the full moon and/or new moon, and then, at the other two quarters, to visualise receiving.

I realised that this could have a placebo effect, that in thinking some outside force was coming to our aid we would feel that we were no longer alone in our mission. It might, I supposed, propel us unconsciously to make greater effort. But then I also knew that once one became aware of one's ability to *make* things happen in this way, one had to simply *let it happen.*

To make sure coincidence or other incidental or accidental occurrences were eliminated, I decide to programme with the moon phases for a very materialistic thing; one over which I had absolutely no influence or control. I decided on winning money. As I had never gambled, done the pools, or owned premium bonds, it seemed a good test. It was almost as if I were saying, *"Try to make this happen when there's no possible way that it can."*

For my visual outgoing force, I pictured an express train going away from me into the distance. On every carriage window was the word, *money, money, money.* On the quarter moons I pictured the postman arriving with it. (From what I have read it was suggested that you picture some kind of force coming towards you, but my mind didn't seem to want to do that, so I stuck with the postman - having first seen the train carrying the mail at high speed towards my home town).

A few weeks later, my mother, who lives with us, won a considerable amount of money on a premium bond. I loved the humour of it. I hadn't actually pictured the money coming to *me*, but to the house. I didn't honestly need or want the money, so it was a wonderful piece of evidence that it did work - though not exactly as I had expected.

I decided to make my next attempt a greater challenge. I practise as a hypnotherapist, but at that time the BMA did not recognise us as a professional body, and doctors were not allowed to refer patients to us. So I programmed for recognition and success in my work. A short time after this I was invited to speak to the post graduate doctors of our local hospital! I have since gone on to teach at adult education colleges on the subject of the unconscious mind, and, as you may know, also to write on the subject. I think I can safely say that my programming worked.

Since that time I have continued to use the system and it has never failed me. My students are amazed and delighted when I introduce them to this. Sometimes they make quite simple requests, sometimes they want to do something really big, like selling a house that has been on the market for two years. It makes no difference, you can ask for anything. It may well work as successfully without linking in with the moon phases, but I have never tried this. I found that using the moon phases is a good discipline.

For those of you who have a religious background, you will recall being told: *Our Father knows all your needs - you only have to ask.* If only we truly believed this!

The creator, God, the life force, call it what you will, has resulted in all that we know, and much that is beyond our senses. It all belongs to us - for we are part of it - so we can have it if we want. I believe that once we have learned how to handle our materialistic world in the best possible way, then we move to higher aspirations and become much more spiritual. But we have to start at the beginning, and so have to learn to handle properly that which is available to us on a materialistic plane. It is all part of our growth. Use what you receive in a bad or negative way and it will have no long-term beneficial effects, of this I am convinced.

Not all things are as immediate as my first few experiences in programming were. You may have to continue to programme over several months, sometimes even years, before anything begins to happen. Everything coming to us at once is not good for us. We need learning experiences, we need to understand the way in which we take our place in our universe.

When I wanted to get my first book published, I programmed for months without getting any direct results. During this time I tried various avenues which included being rejected by nearly two dozen publishers. This resulted in me deciding to publish myself. Six months later the printers, (who also happened to be publishers), said that they would like to publish my children's stories. And so the whole area of my life as a writer developed. I see now that this needed to move slowly for I had much to learn. It also enabled me to keep control of my self-help books which turned out to be the best way of doing things, and so I continue to publish in the way that I believe is best for my readers and for me.

Not convinced? Well, at least give it a try. A step by step exercise follows in programming with the moon phases that can be used by anyone.

Programming with the Moon Phases

Exercise Three - Stage One

Note this is done at the full moon - check with your calendar. It can also be repeated with the new moon.

1. Make yourself comfortable, relax and close your eyes. This can be done at night before you go to sleep if you choose.
2. Think of what you want for a few moments. Picture it.

3. Now visualise an outgoing force going to get you what you want. This can be a jet plane, an arrow, a train - anything that seems appropriate to you is okay.

Stage Two - this time with the quarter moon.

1. Again, relax and close your eyes and think of what it is that you have programmed for - picture it.
2. Now see it coming to you. Using a force of some kind bringing it to you.

Note: I have pictured golden sovereigns pouring into my lap; something being washed up on the shore at my feet; a telegram arriving. So I don't always go along with the *force* idea.

I find it helpful to think about my programming from time to time in a relaxed, confident way, *knowing* that it will come when it is right for me. It makes it easier to focus if we choose something simple to visualise. Simplicity in thought somehow seems to help transmit more readily the frequency of the thought vibrations that are going to have an effect. (Rather like radio waves being picked up by a receiver - though this is oversimplifying the process).

When you truly become aware that you are part of the **Oneness of the Universe**, *there is **no** separation.* You are part of everything and can know everything and be anything. It is what spiritual people see as an awareness of the Universal Consciousness. But understanding, at this stage, is not essential to programming, so go ahead. I would be very interested to hear of your results.

GOOD HEALTH

Where Does It All Start?

Only yesterday found me sitting next to a charming little girl on a long aeroplane flight and the experience made me aware of how much our health is in our own hands.

I played various games with the child to help pass away the long hours. I noticed that her right hand was quite badly deformed and how well she had adapted to using the other for tasks we can only accomplish by using both hands. Half-way through the flight she paused to use an inhaler - she also had a breathing problem. All this had done nothing to diminish her confidence; she was a bright, attractive child with a very positive attitude towards life.

As the flight came to an end, she held out her good hand to shake mine. I longed to hug her, but the quiet dignity with which she bade me farewell made me aware that she was sharing something very special with me.

One could have said that she was just unlucky to be born that way and how wonderful it was that she had turned her disadvantages to her advantage. But it made me think afresh of our own responsibility, not just to ourselves, but also to others, in the way we conduct our lives. Air pollution, water contamination, insecticides, are all man's responsibility. Much of our good health and well-being, we now know, is dependent upon what man allows to happen or creates in his ignorance or greed.

Your Health in Your Hands

How often do you find yourself complaining about your health? Headaches, stomach ulcers, spastic colon, migraines - these, and many more symptoms are directly linked to stress. It is the biggest single factor in sickness and disease. When your body is stressed you cannot function properly.

The national health service and private charities pour billions into research, attempting to find cures, prevention and better medication, when all the time the biggest killer - either directly or indirectly - is stress. About this they have, until recently, been strangely silent. How often does your doctor advise you in reducing stress? How often does he, instead, write out a prescription for some drug?

Remember Exercise Two in this book on relaxation? Do it every day for fifteen minutes. It will **not** be a waste of time but a worthwhile investment.

The way we live, eat, breathe, sleep, move, all have an effect on our health.

Do you honestly exercise as much as you should? Not enough time? It's **your life** we are talking about.

Human beings are still animals, and animals do not exercise for the sake of it. Enough food, shelter and whatever exertion is necessary to ensure safety and reproduction is all the animal is interested in. This is all animals need to do in their natural environment. But we don't live naturally any more; we don't have to run to catch our food, or fight physically, nor do we need to expend energy searching for fuel. We have transport to move us around, escalators to carry us up and down buildings, water pumped to our houses, chairs to sit on in offices, newspapers and telephones to communicate information. We *need* to take exercise outside our normal existence and this requires effort, personal motivation and self discipline.

What happens when you arrive home from work? It has been one hell of a day and all you want to do is flop down in front of the television. But if you are committed to going out - perhaps to evening classes or a visit to a friend, you do feel better after making the effort and motivating yourself to follow through your commitment.

The same applies to exercise. Once you do it, you feel better. This is why people get hooked on working out at the gym. Exercise gets the adrenaline flowing and that gives you a 'high' naturally. Much safer than taking drugs to give you a 'lift', and far more beneficial.

You owe it to yourself to get fit and stay fit.

Stop the convenience junk food, too much alcohol and cigarettes. Eat vegetables and fresh fruit. Avoid processed foods. Too much of anything is bad for you - so remember, *everything in moderation.*

The exception is cigarettes - none at all is the direct route to a healthier way of living.

Staying healthy does not depend on luck. It depends on *us* at every level. From individual effort to political decisions world-wide, our health is in our own hands. *It is our responsibility.*

Whatever health or physical disadvantages you may have been born with, you can improve your state. It is possible to do exercises from a wheelchair. There are many world famous sportsmen and women who have achieved great success though they are without legs or arms, asthmatic, or epileptic.

One of my most moving experiences has been to watch the sporting events on television of those in wheelchairs.

Feeling ill is often used as an escape. It results in people feeling sorry for us. People are nice to you when you are ill; they don't expect anything from you if you are frail or suffer from some incurable 'illness'. We can remember, as children, how nice people were to us when we were ill - hopefully we didn't get away with being 'poorly' too often.

If you have been using this guise - it may well be that you have done so unconsciously, unable to face the world or cope with its challenges - try to recognise the behaviour pattern and determine to do better. Don't let the weaker part of you get away with it. Being an invalid, or claiming some disability, limits your life and prevents you from getting the best out of living.

Most of us never realise our full potential simply because we don't believe we are capable of more than we are doing. Often this comes from negative conditioning during our childhood. A recent survey showed that ninety percent of the instructions given to children are negative.

If you want to be lucky you have to recognise that it lies within your own control. Say good-bye to past experiences, good-bye to negative thinking; the past need have no influence over you in your present life or in your future once you choose to take control and deal with those things that have been holding you back.

My first book, Going Back, written with Frederick Brayshay, tells what happened to him as a child where he experienced rejection, adoption, and hardship. He was placed in a home for waifs and strays, evacuated, denied contact with his blood mother when he finally located her - yet he firmly declares, "It is all too easy to blame everything on someone else. As adults we must take responsibility for our own actions."

It is up to you!

Accidents

You could be forgiven for thinking that accidents, at least, come under the heading of 'bad luck'. After all, you can't help it if the bus you are in hits a wall, or the dog next door suddenly decides to take a bite out of your leg, or you accidentally spill some boiling water over your hand. Or can you?

The truth is that most accidents can be avoided. I might almost go so far as to say *all* accidents can - but you probably aren't ready yet to go that far. After some practice, following the guide lines given in this book, and actually getting results - well then, maybe you will.

Road accidents are those that spring most readily to mind. How can you prevent them? The law has gone a long way to help. The sad truth is that people break the very laws that are made to protect them. The majority of accidents occur because people drive too fast, this is especially so in poor road conditions. One *does* need much more distance in which to stop when the road surface is wet; fog *does* diminish visual distance; and if we drive more slowly we can anticipate people doing thoughtless dangerous things. When children are around we need to drive *much more slowly*. Could you stop if a dog was round the next bend, or a cow had wandered onto the highway? You should be able to if you are driving safely.

Being in a hurry is one of the greatest causes of accidents. Whether we are out shopping, making dinner, using tools at work, in the house or garden, being in too much of a hurry often results in injury.

Distraction, allowing one's mind to be diverted or involved in daydreaming, causes us to do needlessly dangerous things too, or may prevent us from noticing what is happening. We ought to be sufficiently alert to notice the gate swinging on its hinges, the tractor driver who has lost control, the saucepan about to boil over.

Think of the last accident you either witnessed, heard about, or were involved in. Could it have been avoided?

When you become more *aware* of your world and environment you will *naturally* make the right decisions, and take the necessary precautions.

Getting something like flu is often due to neglect - taking care of yourself and dealing with stress can prevent the immune system from being depleted. You didn't catch flu *by accident*, it wasn't your *bad luck*. Of course you may have *needed* to have flu, to legitimately allow yourself to take a few days off; when you need to escape the pressure of work or people, flu can be very useful. But there are better ways of dealing with things, you don't *have* to be ill.

Next time you are involved in an accident - and it can be anything, from cutting your finger peeling vegetables to hitting a tree with your car - ask yourself why it happened and how you could have prevented it.

We are all too ready to blame accidents on someone or something else. "The darned dog shouldn't have been lying in the doorway" or "how was I to know he'd left his bicycle there?" *We should have looked.*

Learning to tune into your world, to be more aware, allows you to have a special way of knowing - it accounts for the stories we hear of people who, at the last moment, decide not to take *that* flight and then the plane crashes.

Meditation, self-hypnosis, prayer, and lucid-dreaming, are all routes you may take to a deeper awareness of your place in the world.

LUCKY IN LOVE

This Thing Called Love

One of the best bits of luck a person can have is in getting the right partner - or is it?

We choose a partner for life with very little experience, wisdom, or the knowledge of what is best for us.

What we do make our decisions on, is something to do with unconscious recognition. We experience a need, and along comes someone who, in some way, fulfils that need. This may be someone who makes us feel important, safe, special; it may even be someone we can dominate or manipulate in a way that gives us power or control. We feel a powerful emotional response to that person and believe we are in love. Often those feelings do develop into a lasting partnership, other times they simply do not.

Sometimes we can choose what proves to be exactly the wrong person for us long-term, but at that moment in time is the one person with whom we feel we can survive. This is seen when a girl, whose father is physically violent, marries a man who subsequently also knocks her around. "Extraordinary!" onlookers might declare. But she had learned how to survive in such an environment. She was, most probably, following the pattern of response learned from unconscious observation of her mother.

The same sort of thing frequently happens with an alcoholic father; although at first the new young husband may *seem* different, after a year or two he, just like dad, begins to drink far too much. Had the girl unconsciously recognised this potential? Was it necessary to her survival? We are certainly very complex creatures. The heartening truth is, that once we do recognise what is happening - when we apply 'awareness' at a higher level - we can recognise what is right and wrong for us and make the best decisions for our happiness and well-being.

A good relationship, which we may call lucky, often results from doing things naturally, and requires no deliberate choosing or assessing; for some, attaining a perfect partner is part of their spiritual growth process.

Thousands of people go through many relationships, testing their feelings, learning, moving on, until they find the one who they feel is *meant* for them. Problems arise when a person begins to panic and fears they will never find the right partner. Then they settle for what seems like the best that is available to them. It can work, but usually lacks the depth of commitment and communication that could have been theirs.

But suppose the opportunity doesn't arise to meet someone who is compatible with you - someone you can really fall in love with? Suppose you just don't meet the right partner for you? Well, we do still have some control. If you pursue interests that are important to you, you are much more likely to meet someone with similar interests and this is a good foundation on which to build a relationship. Perhaps it will lead to love, and even if it doesn't, you have probably made a friend for life.

The Way You Are

Being shy, finding it difficult to communicate, or having a poor opinion of yourself, will all limit your choices. Remember, you can change and widen your horizons. Don't ever think someone wouldn't love you because of your looks - it is the way we make people feel inside that draws them to us and sustains a relationship. Those who radiate happiness are never short of friends or lovers.

The other day I handed a friend a photograph of us on holiday the previous summer. "Oh my goodness! How old I look! What a mess my hair was in!" she gasped. She totally failed to notice how *happy* we both looked.

Feeling happy in a relationship is a good yard stick by which to measure how durable it will be. When you feel you can truly be yourself, and that you are accepted the way you are, you won't need *luck* to make it last.

How a Relationship Can Work

We can learn a lot by pausing to take a look at how a relationship starts and develops. Let us choose a loving one that possesses all the right intentions - *it is meant to last for life*. We will call our hero in this little story, Joe.

Joe, who is 'head over heels in love', is quite incapable of stepping back and asking the following questions:

1. How much do we have in common - culture, upbringing, education, beliefs, friends, hobbies?
2. How much do we share?
3. How much am I prepared to put into making it work?
4. Do I care enough about her to make permanent changes in my life?
5. Why do I want to spend the rest of my life with her?
6. Can what I now feel last?

These are the sort of things our hero ought to be asking himself, but the 'feelings' of being in love are far too powerful. Chemistry, hormones, energies, unconscious responses to past programming all play their part - driven along by them he has only one thought, *he must have this person*.

The initial euphoria may last a few months, it could go on for several years, but eventually the humdrum routine of everyday life inevitably levels it off to ordinary living.

Does our hero begin to spend more and more time away from home, at the club or fishing perhaps? Does he feel resentment when his wife has to give more and more of her time to their children?

Does she brush him aside when he tries to be attentive because there are more important things to do? Does she stop dressing up to please him? Does he stop courting her, and does sex become routine with those special moments overlooked? After all, he's tired and has to get up at six thirty the next morning.

But Joe had unconsciously made the right decisions and followed his natural feelings when he chose his partner - no one taught him how to be a good husband or how to understand women, it seemed to happen by chance that all the right ingredients went into his choice.

There was, however, one essential 'thing' that Joe did do - he loved with all his heart. His wife could not help but respond. His total commitment caused an effect - her loving response. Joe was so loveable she was compelled to love him in return.

A Positive Viewpoint

So often we fail because we believe there is nothing we can do. If you have lost a loved one who, at some point stopped returning your affections, now, in a quiet moment, examine that relationship. It could have been a necessary learning ground for you. Perhaps you weren't able to ask yourself the right questions at that time; you may have been unable to communicate with your deep-down sense of *knowing* what is right for you.

Sometimes, marriage or a relationship, is used as an act of defiance or a means of escape and does not last. If this proves to be your experience, rest assured, you can do better next time.

We know that the unconscious mind can influence much of what we do and experience - it also sometimes ensures that in a relationship we make choices which, on the surface seem to be bad ones, but are necessary for our development.

Let us now take a look at a completely different kind of story: This one demonstrates how much is dependent on the way we see things.

How a Viewpoint Changes our Perception

A group of men were gathered at the bar of their local pub. They had discussed at some length the last performance of the village football team; they had agreed on the diabolical mess the current government was making of the subsidies to farmers, and had reached a hearty discussion on a travel film most of them happened to have watched on TV the previous night.

"Drink up," Chris said. "I'll get the next round and then I must be off. Liz will be waiting up for me."

As he gathered the glasses and walked to the bar, he failed to notice the exchanged glances and raised eyebrows of his companions.

"It's pathetic!" Des declared as soon as the door had closed behind him. "Fancy allowing himself to be tied to her apron strings like that!"

"It's his third marriage too," Eric put in. "You'd think he had learned a thing or two by now. No woman would have me at her beck and call like that - especially not when I'm out drinking with my mates."

Charlie sighed. "Chris thinks that he's the luckiest man alive."

"How come?" Des queried. "With two wives dead and a third that nags him to be home by ten! I wouldn't call that luck. Unless you'd like to call it **bad** luck."

"If you asked him, he'd tell you that he had ten marvellous years with his first wife and fourteen with the second. He sees himself as lucky to have had such good experiences," Charlie explained. "And he's grateful to have lived with three different lovely ladies."

For a moment they all fell silent. Eric was thinking about his Sal. If he dared to wake her when he got home he'd get a right earful of abuse.

Des's wife was out herself so she wouldn't notice what time *he* arrived home. He doubted if she'd be bothered if he stayed out all night. Since she had started French lessons all she did was drift around practising her gobbly-de-gook on him. If he tried to get friendly she brushed his hands aside saying, "Not now, Des. I'm memorising my French verbs."

Charlie had never married. Sometimes he found himself envying the others - especially Chris. For all the leg-pulling, Chris had someone to go home to who cared about him. Fancy a wife who waited up for you; making you a cup of tea, cuddling up to you in bed! But Charlie had always been too scared of the commitment. Suppose it hadn't worked?

The best ingredient to take into a marriage/partnership/relationship is *love in your heart* - real love, demanding nothing in return, wanting the recipient's happiness more than all else. Love is out-flowing, it doesn't ask, *what is there in this for me?* But rather, *what can I put into this relationship? How can I make it richer, fuller, happier, deeper, exciting, adventurous?* All this need not be thought of at a conscious level, but it is there, deep-down inside. Anything and everything is possible when you put in the right ingredients. Remember that a relationship must include two people - and both must be fully present for this to work. With the best will in the world a relationship needs the total commitment of two people if it is to last for life.

When Love is Not Returned

In some cases the person we fall in love with has done nothing to warrant our affections. Just by being, they can initiate very powerful responses. It is not through bad luck that they fail to respond. The relationship was never meant to be.

A young man or women can believe themselves to be very much in love without actually knowing anything about the other person as a 'real' human being. The feelings are prompted by an invisible, unconscious, motivating force. Perhaps they are not ready for a realistic relationship; perhaps bad experiences of a past one has made them withdraw to a safe distance, and yet, because they still have a need to love they do so from afar.

Sometimes love can become so powerful a force it results in obsessive behaviour. Totally against the will of the other person, who quite genuinely 'doesn't want to know', the lover pours his/her unwanted attentions onto the object of his/her love. They are using the person to fulfil a need which has nothing to do with a real two-way relationship.

Sex

It is an interesting fact that when men get together and talk about sex, they usually focus upon their conquests and above-average performances; when women discuss sex they more often talk about what is wrong in their love-life or what they don't enjoy.

"If you get someone who is good in bed you are bloody lucky!" Dennis commented to his cronies. "Most women don't want to know you after a couple of years, or as soon as the kids come along."

He spoke with some bitterness, having had two disastrous marriages.

I overheard the conversation but could say nothing. His wife had been a friend of mine and I had listened to her 'soul searching' for many an hour before she finally decided to end things.

"If only he would just love me sometimes. But it's all sex or nothing," she sighed. "I've reached the stage where I can't bear him to touch me."

Of course we do have individual needs and they do differ. Often the problem lies in our not being able to communicate them.

There is one thing worth exploring that has a lot more to do with the difference between men and women and enjoying sex than just luck. What most women need and respond to, what leads to the physical enjoyment, is the gentle approach, being made to feel they are loved for themselves. For most men the preliminaries are the road to the act of intercourse itself which allows them to experience the ultimate climax. Perhaps they need to realise that the preliminaries should start long before they reach the bedroom, that loving care demonstrated throughout the evening creates a willing response and ultimate joyful participation for both.

I am not suggesting this is the only solution to a better sex life, but it is one route often ignored or not understood.

Tacking sex on to the end of a busy day does nothing to value it or make it feel special. Sex, such a wonderful expression of love and unity, is like a beautiful rose, it needs to be appreciated, looked at, approached with a sense of awe for its uniqueness. Every time it is experienced it holds potential life.

A True Story

When I was a child, returning from Sunday School with my sister, we would often stop off at my aunt's house for a drink and to say 'hello'.

The door was almost always locked. This did nothing to deter us, we knew that she always kept a spare key on the mangle in the garage.

My aunt used to call us 'little perishers'

Opening the back door, we would stomp through the house calling our greetings. Climbing the stairs we usually found my aunt and uncle in their bedroom peering over the sheets at us from their big double bed.

My aunt would call us 'little perishers' and send us off downstairs to make a pot of tea.

I never had the faintest idea *why* they always went to bed on a Sunday afternoon. Only when I was married with a family of my own did I recall, and remember with a smile, what an *inconvenience* our visits must have been.

When my aunt and uncle were quite old they still held hands under the tea table, and could be found kissing in the kitchen as they washed up together.

They had recognised the importance of sex and gave it the time and respect it deserved in their marriage. It never entered their heads to put their wonderful relationship down to **luck**.

SUPERSTITIONS AND LUCKY NUMBERS

Fear

In order to fully benefit from the knowledge and new insights offered in this book, it is essential that you confront your fears and deal with them.

Take the time to recognise where fear has been masked by making luck accountable for failure and negative experiences. Some folk unconsciously construct their own obstacles by blaming luck. They believe that if they are too successful, bad luck is sure to follow.

Pride is said to come before a fall, and yet there is nothing wrong with feeling proud, so long as you bear in mind that your talents are gifts, freely given to you at birth, and nothing to do with personal effort.

Many of our self-created barriers to success come under the label of 'Superstitions'. Do they exist, or are they contrived restrictions handed down from pagan days intended to control? Or are they used to explain the 'unexplainable'?

Dealing with Fear

Exercise Four - Dealing with Unnecessary Fears

1. Make yourself comfortable in a place where you will not be disturbed. Close your eyes and breathe deeply for a few minutes. Notice the rhythm of your breathing and relax with your breathing.

2. Now mentally check over your body. Allow each part of you to relax: your toes and feet; your calf muscles and thigh muscles; your stomach muscles; your chest, body and back muscles . . . Relax the muscles in your scalp, your face, your jaw, your neck and shoulder muscles. Imagine all the tension from your neck

and shoulders flowing down your arms and out through the tips of your fingers; let your arms and hands relax. Return your attention to your breathing, take a very deep breath, hold it, and then let go and relax completely.

3. Think about your fear; the kind of fear that gets in the way but is not essential to your survival. Name some of those things that make you anxious, perhaps they cause tension in your stomach muscles or neck muscles; they may cause you to sweat or to get migraine. Because you are now relaxed you can think about your fears in a calm, detached way. Do some of your fears cause you embarrassment? Do they prevent you from doing things you ought to be able to do, or things you would like to do? Does your fear hold you back from success? What are you afraid of? It may be the reaction of other people; their criticism or rejection - perhaps you think you will lose friends or that others will deceive you and that you will no longer know whom you can trust. Are you afraid that you will not be able to cope with success or material gain? Do you believe that you don't deserve good things to happen to you?

4. Decide now to set yourself free from those fears you no longer want or need. Imagine rolling all those fears into a bright red ball, keep rolling the ball (like a ball of wool); you draw them out of you, winding and winding until there are none left inside.

5. Picture a table in front of you and place the ball on that table. Watch the ball, see it change to a soft pink colour; see it grow smaller and smaller. The colour becomes fainter as the ball continues to reduce in size. The ball disappears completely.

6. Notice how relaxed and peaceful you feel now that you have let go of the fears you no longer need.

Note: Don't worry if you find this difficult at first. Repeat this visual exercise daily until you do really feel calm and in control of your own feelings.

Superstitions

If you are from England, having a black cat cross your path is said to be very lucky. If you come from Germany it must pass from right to left in order to bring good luck. Should you be unfortunate enough to be there when it crosses from left to right - better look out! This spells bad luck for sure.

I only heard of this difference in the black cat superstition recently; it is a good demonstration of how ridiculous most superstitions are. Naturally you are not going to walk under a ladder if you can avoid it, the man above could slip, and you might find yourself with a pot of paint down the back of your neck.

The origin of most superstitions has become lost with time, but that does nothing to prevent us from keeping them alive. Wearing black at a funeral was, at one time, intended to keep evil spirits out, but how many still believe in evil spirits or know the origin of wearing black? Yet still it is worn at funerals.

Do you remember being told that if you crossed someone on the stairs one of you would have twins? It makes you wonder what happened to all those multiple births, doesn't it?

When I decided to include a chapter on superstitions in this book, I made some local enquiries and discovered all kinds of superstitions I had previously not known. Did you know that changing your bed sheets on a Friday was supposed to bring you bad luck? I am hard pushed to imagine where that one came from. And did you know that a tea leaf floating on your tea means a stranger is going to call? Now most of us use tea bags I suppose we have lost this prior warning facility! And do you know that if you put your sweater on inside-out you must wear it that way or bad luck will follow you all the day?

I can, in a way, understand how people came to build superstitions around the moon. It does have a very powerful influence on our planet. But why must you not look at the new moon through glass, and why are we supposed to turn our money over when we see the new moon?

An elderly friend told me that when he was a boy, if they saw a white horse, they all drew a cross on the toes of their boots. He never even knew why. It was just something they did.

I notice that children still avoid walking on cracks in the pavement. Well, in days past perhaps the paving wasn't very reliable, and one *might* trip over a broken edge, so there may have been a good reason originally for that superstition.

Spilled salt on the table, I am told, used to indicate war. By throwing a pinch over your shoulder - and it had to be the right one - you could avert such disaster. Now I had always thought that it came from the days when salt was as valuable a commodity as water, and returning it to the ground ensured that you would never be without.

I find the superstitious belief of salt quite interesting, having seen on television a programme where a tribe of people began to produce blind and visually disabled children. This, the natives said, only happened after the white man came. Further investigation proved that the white man provided salt, and the locals no longer had to traipse miles to get it. What no one knew, was that the salt they fetched contained iodine which was essential to their limited diet, and the salt the white man brought contained none.

One can easily see how *that* could become the basis for a superstition.

So why do we, as an educated race of people, go on perpetuating these stories of punishment and disaster? Could it be that we have been conditioned into focusing only on certain aspects of the myths? I am sure that you know if you focus totally on one thing, you fail to read other signs.

Something terrible happens whenever I wear that green dress, I heard a relative say. Did she honestly believe nothing ever went wrong when she wore any other dress? But it only took a couple of times when she spilt something on it, and then a phone call to say someone was in hospital, and she was convinced it was due to the dress. In a primitive way, it took away the responsibility. And we do like to blame something or someone when things go wrong.

Well, of course, we know it's silly. But oh, so hard to stop!

Only by becoming consciously aware of those occasions when we allow ourselves to be influenced by superstitious beliefs, and turning our focus on to the positive times when nothing bad happened, can we hope to break the cycle.

What of gypsies and predictions? How often has a warning come true for you? Genuine gypsies live much closer to nature than most of us. We have lost much of our ability to tune into nature by the very way in which we now live. Do gypsies have the wisdom to read a face or a palm, or is it something more? The sheer mystery surrounding the life of gypsies - so alien to our own - can breed fear and lead to superstition. Fear overrides common sense and can create the most irrational responses.

Lucky Mascots and Lucky Charms

Once it was a common habit for people to carry a rabbit's foot in their pocket for luck. Barbaric and unhygienic though this may sound, it is still quite often used by many people in the country and by some sports people.

Teddy bears, dolls, cuddly toys, a dog or goat may all be seen to be openly used to bring the owner (or team) good luck.

Many sports people are convinced that unless they have their lucky mascot or follow a special sequence of movements (ritual), that all their efforts will be to no avail; they will fail to achieve success.

You perhaps have, yourself, a small thing - a coin, brooch, certain pen - that you feel does, in some way, ensure that good things will happen to you. You can't explain it, but you feel that way.

By believing something outside of ourselves has an influence, we are opening up to a special power that we feel convinced will come to our aid. We fail to see that it is the conviction of our belief that actually has the effect. Then, of course, if things don't go the way we hoped, we look for something else to blame - *anything*, except the lucky charm! If we blame that and throw it out, we are going to have to rely upon ourselves, and that is often a frightening alternative.

Body Language

Much of what we now do is bred in us. Long ago body language was probably all we had to go on, and we continue to use it unconsciously even after we learn to verbally communicate or understand the spoken word. After years and years of communicating through the use of words, body language is said to still be the most powerful communicator for more than seventy percent of the time. It tells us when to trust a person or when they are lying.

If you take the time to observe body language, you will know when to believe what you are being told. Often what people say with their mouths is totally contradicted by their body language. Watch a politician on television and you will see what I mean: he or she may be saying something in the affirmative, but their head is moving to and fro in very definite *no* movements.

A dozen things will tell us not to believe what we are hearing: an unnatural stiffness of the body, tension around the mouth, the unblinking eye lids or an inability to meet your gaze; the voice *sounds* different and the hand movements do not support what is being said.

A good card player uses all this to his advantage; reading the body language of the other players tells him far more than what they attempt to portray. Hand gestures will tell him when the other player is attempting to disguise something, when he is going to take a risk, when he tries to portray a lie, or attempts to disguise one.

It has been noted that a card player who is smoking will blow the smoke upwards if he has been dealt a good hand; if he has a poor hand he is likely to blow it downwards. A deliberate poker face may be adopted to hide the player's feelings, but the rest of the body will be a give-away if you take the time to learn to read the signals.

Remember also, if you are into card playing for pleasure or money, that your own body language will, to a certain extent, be read unconsciously by others - so you can use it to your advantage.

Getting Closer To Reality

The wonderful thing about good things happening to you naturally, is that you don't have to use pretence or guile. You don't have to study for years or pay out a lot of money in training either - you simply have to tune in to your inner self and let good fortune happen. You only need to be attentive in order that you do not miss those signs when they are given to you.

So, do away with superstitions and open the door to the real wonders of the world.

Those things that are of real value to you are available in abundance. Knowing this and opening yourself to it, you become part of the rhythm of life, part of the 'whole'.

Example

I may think, *I could do with a window cleaner,* and the next morning one knocks on the door enquiring if I need his services. I could have asked around or placed an advert in the local shop window and got the same results. But it is so much more fun doing it this way, and I can be sure the man is right for the job.

I know this happens. It happens to me, over and over again.

The other day I was wondering how I could get my books into an area where there was a bigger range of customers. I know very little about selling books and to pursue this objective I would have to do a lot of research which would be time consuming and expensive. Two days later the telephone rang, one of the airport book shop suppliers was asking me if they could have my books to sell at their terminals.

Such experiences make one very humble and exhilarated at the same time. The completeness of the universe is so complex, and yet at the same time so beautifully simplistic. We only have to believe and all things are made possible.

By telling you this, I am not suggesting that you sit back and do nothing. I am extremely industrious and do get on with things when that seems the right way to go about achieving, but I'm not averse to a little help from outside (which really comes from inside - if you get my meaning).

Having had the thought, don't worry it like a terrier with a rag doll. There is no need to become dramatic, intense or to deliberately try to make things come about - it doesn't work that way. Just *allow* it to happen. And do let me know how you get on.

Numbers - Lucky or Unlucky?

Is seven a lucky number for you? Or nine, or twenty four? Do you believe a certain number will help you to win the raffle, or a holiday of a lifetime? If the number has come up more than twice you are probably convinced.

How many people believe thirteen is an unlucky number? How many refuse to travel on Friday the thirteen? Perhaps you are one of those people who seem to have all the evidence you need to support this belief of disastrous consequences if you travel on Friday the thirteenth.

Hundreds of thousands of people fly, travel to work by bus, train and car on Friday the thirteenth and nothing untoward happens to them. There is no evidence of more accidents happening on the thirteenth than on any other date in the year, and yet still the fear continues to control many people.

Does their negative thinking really *make* something bad happen to them? Or have they been focusing solely on one, or maybe two occasions when something did go wrong. And have they never been involved in a misfortune on any other date?

I am not suggesting that certain numbers may *not* have a special significance for you. You probably visualise them in such a way that your imaging has an effect. If this is so - and it is reported that it does happen for some people - either *you* are making it happen, or you are being given a preview 'outside of time'. Just keep on doing it, but make sure the numbers have a positive effect - don't leave it to luck!

A friend recently told me how thirteen was a lucky number for her. She met her husband on the thirteenth, was married on the thirteenth, had her daughter on the thirteenth and lived in a house numbered thirteen. Of course this 'good luck' associated with the number depended on her viewpoint, had she seen the marriage and daughter as a disaster or mistake, she would have had a very different feeling about the number thirteen. But she used a very positive viewpoint and enjoyed the feeling.

Much of what we experience is dependent on how we see things. By taking a positive viewpoint on life you are bound to get the best results. You might say that you can't help but feel lucky when everything is seen in this light.

USING YOUR DREAMS

What Dreams Tell Us

I have referred to Edgar Cayce and his ability to dream things that were to happen in the future and how he used that knowledge both for gain and growth. He did, however, always insist that what was important, was the person's motive. Let us bear this in mind as we investigate how our dreams can be used by us.

How can we use *our* dreams in a way that helps us to a more profitable way of living? We all dream, though many who fail to recall their dreams, may deny this. Dreams give us the opportunity to communicate with our inner self. While the ego takes a back-seat, the unconscious part of us is active in dreaming; it helps us to identify and resolve problems.

Dreams can be very rewarding and enlightening - it all depends on how we relate to insight in this way and what we do with it.

Dreams give us the opportunity to form a relationship between the waking ego and the deeper inner part of our being.

The theme behind your dreams, the way you are conducting yourself within your dreams, the problems you are repeatedly having to confront, all help you to see how better you can develop at a conscious level. If you find yourself fleeing from situations, ask yourself what it is in your life that you are failing to confront, or to deal with. When obstacles present themselves, they are a dream level message telling you that you need to deal with something or someone that is preventing you from progressing with your life.

A dream often shows us that we have a problem, but not how to solve it. This then is where we have to make a commitment to dealing with the problem at a conscious level. Dreams give us the opportunity to bring our unconscious processing into positive action, it therefore seems a pity when we ignore them, or fail to recall them.

Learning to recall dreams is not difficult. When you have decided that you do want to know about this other level of yourself, keep a note book beside the bed and as soon as you awake write down any notes - however brief - that will help you to remember your dreams later in the day when you choose to consider them.

Dreams are not a result of luck or coincidence, they are the product of mental, creative energy at a different level. Learning to record your dreams, to understand them and use them productively, can give you control and help you to become the best you are capable of becoming. They open up a new awareness and understanding.

Creative Dreaming

Creative dreaming is not new. Scientists, artists, writers, sports people, and many more, have been using it for centuries. Because creativity comes from that part of the brain which does not use logic - the right hemi-sphere - it is necessary for us to learn how to pass over problems to that part of the brain when we go to sleep and let an idea incubate.

Often our logical way of processing an idea misses out completely on a unique solution. We get too used to thinking in one way and find it impossible to see things from a different viewpoint.

Our dream world has no such limitations. If you pause and recall a dream, you will notice that you never asked the question during that dream, "Is this possible?" And so the most bizarre things can happen and be allowed to develop with no restrictive thoughts, as the mind searches for solutions.

Have you ever woken up with a bright idea, or the solution to a problem? It just seems to come to you from nowhere. On other occasions the idea or solution, having incubated during the night, will suddenly present itself in the middle of the day, completely out of context with what you are doing at that moment.

The trouble is that if we don't pay attention to our dreams; they often drift back into our unconsciousness and are lost to us.

Here is a method I have used over many years to help me that I find works very well. It may require some initial practice but is well worth the effort. Remember that very little of real value comes without personal effort.

Exercise Five - Creative and Insight Dreaming

1. Before going to sleep, spend a few minutes thinking over your day. Note anything to which you had emotional responses. e.g. nearly missing the bus for work; an argument with a friend; a piece of music that made you feel sad. Also note things that you have seen but have not had time to give conscious thought to. (The unconscious mind will often use these in a symbolic way).

2. Now think about what it is that needs creative thought. Your project for this dream work could be: how to make more money; how to present a talk in an original way; how to apply for a new job; how to improve your business; how to produce something that is unique; how to solve a problem.

3. Use a phrase or sentence that encompasses this thought. Repeat it to yourself as you drift into sleep. e.g. *I need a new and exciting job.* (It's similar to using a mantra in meditation.)

4. Think about your dream immediately on waking and make any appropriate notes

Note: Don't worry if you can't remember your dreams, this will come with practice. It is not always necessary to remember at a conscious level. The way you conduct yourself will probably be evidence enough that *something* happened while you were sleeping that is beneficial to you.

If you do decide to use this method for trying to dream lucky numbers, proceed with caution, often wistful thoughts can be so powerful that we mistake them for the real thing.

Using your dreams can be very inspirational, revealing, creative, and informative about your own mental state; dreams can reveal mental blocks, and, once having recognised this, one can set about removing them.

Dream Symbols

As we become used to recording our dreams we also become more adept at interpretation. Often answers come in the form of symbols. They can give us instant insight, but they can also be very misleading if we fail to interpret them correctly.

Suppose that you have decided to go to the races the next day; as you drift into sleep you think about this and decide you will have one big bet. When you awake you recall a dream where you were planting, and then in the next part of the dream you are harvesting three bright red shiny apples. As you think about this you may interpret the planting as the foundation for your success and the apples as the fruits of your labours. When you read the racing card you see that there is a horse there called Apple Pie - is this the one your dream predicted? Or are you supposed to bet on the third race? Or is it the number of the jockey? Are you being shown that there are three options? With so many choices you would be very foolish to put all your money on one of these. Unless you have a powerful feeling that goes beyond all doubt, it is better to tread cautiously and spend considerable time testing out your dreams. Perhaps you will decide that betting is not the route for you to take after all.

The Words We Use

Words used in common sayings and as puns often appear in our dreams. I had a very strange one once where a situation in the dream I was having sickened me; I tried to vomit, only to cough up tiny green frogs who went hopping about on the path outside my front door. It was only on waking, that I recognised I had a lot of phlegm in my throat and made the connection - *a frog in the throat*! My dream had enabled me to go on sleeping despite the discomfort.

And then, quite some time after, I took another look at my dream. The cause of my feeling sick had been brought about by a friend arriving at the door with twins in a pram wearing identical clothing. In the dream I had thought how *sickening* it was to have everything the same. Now I saw, at another level, that the visitor could have been a projection of myself; that having, in reality, several children and a life that was sickeningly the same, was my real problem.

Dreams often have several functions. A dream may be telling us something about an immediate situation - as with my dream concerning the phlegm in my throat; and an underlying problem we need to deal with - my coping with small children; and a spiritual problem of growth - my need to attend to my inner self.

I dreamt that I had a frog in my throat

Transporting a Thought

I was surprised to discover recently that experiments on dreaming carried out in a dream laboratory showed that some people become telepathic whilst dreaming. An impartial person, focused on a series of images on certain cards, and these images were later reported by the sleeping person to have appeared in his dreams. It happened far too often to be explained away as coincidence.

I have noticed over and over again, that things that we see (or which occur in our everyday lives) to which we do not pay conscious attention, often get used in our sleep. When you recall a dream, you can usually think back and make this connection. This is especially noticeable when there has been something on television to which you have not paid particular attention (this is how subliminal advertising works). Do think about this possibility before interpreting dream symbols and ask yourself if there is a connection.

Working with clients with emotional problems, often reveals that their depression is a response to something seen on television that they have taken on board as a personal experience.

Example

Many years ago I had a difficult client who came for an initial interview. Having discussed a course of therapy he then wrote to say that he wasn't going to go ahead. His letter was not one that left me with feelings of regret - I was rather glad he had changed his mind.

Then, to my surprise, he arrived at the time of his appointment as if he had never written the letter. When I mentioned this, he brushed it to one side and asked me to commence his treatment. His manner was brusque and officious.

That night I had a dream in which I witnessed an aeroplane crash. A temporary enquiry shed was set up near the scene of the accident and I went along to give my report. The enquiry officer was most abrupt; he told me not to give my version but to answer *his* questions. I walked away feeling quite annoyed; after speaking with a friend, I decided that I should return and tell the officer what I thought of the way he conducted things. After all, I was helping him! I didn't *have* to, and I thought his behaviour most inappropriate.

On waking, I thought about this dream and suddenly realised that it represented the situation I was in with my new client. I then saw that if I was going to help him, I had to reverse our roles and take control of the sessions we had together. I had never had this experience with a client before and had failed to notice what was happening. This did work very well, it was what he needed - as an authoritative figure he had found it difficult to ever let someone else take control, and this was partly why he had his problem in relating to other people.

Another interesting thing about that plane crash dream, was that I had been reading about one just before I went to sleep. In itself it was not significant, but my unconscious mind had used it to present to me the problem I needed to address. Had I not realised this I might have focused on the crash as a warning that an accident or disaster of some kind was about to happen.

All this may sound a bit complicated, but with a little practice it soon becomes quite easy to understand your own dreams; it can be very rewarding and gives you a view of your world which has hitherto probably gone unnoticed.

A True Personal Story

One morning, when I went in to attend to my mother, who is almost blind and physically disabled, she told me that she had, that night, experienced a most peculiar dream. "I dreamt that there was something wrong with my foot," she told me. "The doctor who examined it said that although the toes had gone septic, they could be saved and I would not need to have them amputated."

Understanding a little about dreams, I wondered if this was a forewarning. "Let me take a look at your feet," I said.

I found that beneath the toes of one foot, the flesh had become septic and puss was oozing from the broken surface. Immediate attention did indeed prevent amputation.

Another True Story

After speaking one evening in a local hotel, I realised the next morning that the sapphire necklace I had been wearing was not in my bedroom. I recalled the necklace had been irritating my neck, but as I did not want to cause distraction by fiddling with it, I chose to ignore the feeling. Had the clasp broken? I wondered. I phoned the hotel but no one had handed it in. After a much more thorough search I still failed to find the necklace and decided to put in an insurance claim. The night before the cheque arrived I dreamt where the necklace was. The next morning I went to the chest and found it in a small jewellery box amongst some empty ones. The assumption here could be that I had put it there and forgotten doing so; but it was the lady who cleaned the house at that time who had noticed the necklace and put it away for safety, forgetting to tell me.

The insurance brokers were very much surprised when I returned the cheque. They said nothing like that had ever happened to them before!

I relate these two dreams because they *are* personal and I can vouch for them. I am not unique in having such experiences, we all do from time to time.

As dreams and dreamwork are such a big subject and have so many functions, it is not my intention to delve deeply into the subject here. But the exercise given above will give you results that I am sure will prompt you to pursue this fascinating world further.

There are dream workshops and dream groups where people work together at understanding and sharing dream experiences. You may like to follow this up by enquiring at your local library, adult education centre, or local information office.

MANAGEMENT OF SUCCESS

How Things Go Wrong

The saddest thing about success is that most people do not know how to manage it.

Realising your dreams ought to bring great happiness, but all too often people abuse and misuse success.

Almost every day we can read in the papers of people who have become millionaires - usually through their own diligence and efforts - only to lose the lot and declare bankruptcy. Very often the idea of losing everything is so terrifying a concept to them that they divert funds, manipulate accounts and resort to other fraudulent practices to ensure that they won't lose out too drastically when the crash comes. Others commit suicide, or run away, leaving loved ones, to spend their days in isolation in a foreign country.

To lose everything and to learn from that experience is probably the most valuable thing that they will do with their lives. Such an experience could be their greatest asset, but often they fail to see it.

There is *nothing* wrong with possessions, and we all need enough money to ensure security, a roof over our heads and enough food in our bellies.

If you are not mature enough, if you have not grown spiritually, failing to get all that you want can be a blessing.

The inability to manage success is seen repeatedly in the behaviour of TV and film personalities. They appear to have everything - except contentment. Marriages are attempted over and over again with nothing learned. Money buys them everything, except happiness.

Oh! we see the smiling faces turned to the cameras, the confident air of success, the big cars and fabulous houses. It is only later that their true lives, devoid of deep-down lasting joy, are revealed.

Humility

If you succeed in anything, whether it be singing, sport, acting, writing, inventing, science, or accumulating money, it is essential to your stability that you recognise from whence your success came.

Be proud of your industry, your self-discipline and endeavour, but never forget that all you achieve is a result of your talents and gifts.

Your capacity to think, feel, move, speak, see, hear, even to breathe, are all *given* to you. It is well that we remind ourselves of this from time to time, before climbing too eagerly onto the throne of self-importance.

Beautiful models parading the cat-walks, earn a living, not by what they have achieved - although, of course, some personal effort is required - but by the way in which they have evolved from conception.

How often we women concern ourselves with our looks. How slim, shapely, and long are our legs? At eighty plus the only concern is that they will support us until we get back home and can sit down. A thought like that can make you very humble.

But why can't we learn it early on? Well, of course, it's not impossible. But we need to keep reminding ourselves where the roots of our success, at every level, lie.

When your *luck* begins to change - when you take control and discover how much you can help things manifest themselves, please, please, don't boast of such achievements as if you alone are responsible. Consider sharing them humbly with those who also need some 'good luck' to come their way, and give credit to your creator.

Just telling people about something good that has happened to you is a way of sharing. I did this a few weeks ago when several things had gone right for me. They included finding a parking space right outside the shop I had to visit, when I was very short of time; managing to put exactly ten pounds worth of petrol into the car (usually it always goes a few pence over); finding that the first dress I tried on not only fitted perfectly, but was just right for the function I had to attend as speaker; and getting to the checkout at the super store without having to queue. I told the girl cashier of my 'good luck' and to my surprise she called over another girl to pack my groceries for me - that had *never* happened before. She wanted to be part of my lucky day and I felt as if she had enjoyed the experience as much as I had.

Most of us do need to experience materialistic wealth in order to be able to put it in its proper place. Enjoy those things that money or position can give you, be grateful and appreciate the beauty in a piece of china or jewellery, a lovely garden, house or swimming pool. Many things contain the skill and devotion of craftsmen, and the one privileged to own such things should appreciate them. But we also need to appreciate that the true value of life does not lie in money and personal possessions - though they need to be experienced to be seen for what they really are: things that perish and only take priority in the man or woman who never aspires to a higher quality of living.

Through the media we see how many rich people do manage their success in ways that help others. They treat money with respect, using it in positive ways to help children in under developed countries, to set up research clinics for specific diseases, to finance homes for those who need continual care and yet also need to hold on to their independence. The Cheshire Homes for those suffering from multiple sclerosis is one charity that comes to mind where the investment of love and money has had such positive results.

In the Christian bible we are told, *it is easier for a camel to pass through the eye of a needle than for a rich man to enter into the Kingdom of Heaven.* Have you ever wondered why?

Take all that you have from this world and then hand it back. It is only on loan to you, hopefully to use wisely. None of us can take any of our worldly possessions with us when we move beyond this physical existence to whatever lies beyond, and so the best we can hope to do, is to use them wisely while we have them.

Learning from Children

One of my children recently reminded me that *charity begins at home*. He is right. Our first responsibility must be to our families, we should not expect any authority to provide for them unless there are circumstances beyond our control. Also, by over-providing we do them no favour.

Watch the enjoyment of a small child playing with an old saucepan, a heap of sand, a twig, a piece of discarded paper - they don't need expensive toys.

Play with any child, give him your time, talk to him. He would rather a thousand times have your company than be left alone with a room full of toys.

Children can be perfectly happy lying in the grass watching an ant at work - preferably with you alongside. The trouble is that we soon spoil all that by sitting them down in front of a television set.

When I am involved with children, baby-sitting, taking them out for a day, visiting schools, the thing that strikes me, is how much they need to *talk* with you. It makes me wonder how much they talk with adults at home.

What does all this have to do with luck? A good relationship between children and parents does not happen by luck but is the product of years of communication and learning together. Love, discipline and mutual respect are what counts. It is just as well our relationship with our parents and children doesn't depend on luck!

Notice next time you hear someone say how lucky they are to have such a caring son or daughter, or what a marvellous mother or father they have - get to really wondering *why* the relationship is so good and how it came about.

Handling a successful relationship is an ongoing process - it involves commitment. Neglect a relationship, leave all the effort to the other person, and although the 'caring' may still be in evidence, something will soon be felt to be lacking - nurturing is needed.

The Underlying Need to Succeed

I have a friend who, though now in his late forties, is still trying to be successful in an endeavour to fulfil his father's expectations of him. He feels that he doesn't love his father and has lost his respect for him, but he cannot jump off the tread mill. Outwardly it may appear that he is a caring son wanting to please his father - in reality, it is a mixture of guilt, despair and anger that drives him on. He can never satisfy this demanding, garrulous old man. This isn't a loving relationship, but an endless form of slavery to impossible requirements. The son spoke recently to me: "I have to deal with this compulsion to please him, otherwise I'll still be trying, even after he is dead."

This is an example of where success is an impossible goal. What is needed, is that the son learns to manage his own life in the right way and stops trying to live the failed one of his father.

We all learn from what we label as 'our mistakes'. When we see mistakes as positive learning experiences, we set ourselves free from a sense of failure and this enables us to productively use those experiences.

The Unconscious Choice

Although many theories are offered, we don't understand yet what *unconsciousness* means. There are psychoanalysts, psychotherapists, humanists and others who spend years attempting to find the answers. Some believe that unconsciousness is present in our consciousness but that we are simply not aware of it. This seems to make sense when you recognise that experiences and things learned and long forgotten at a conscious level still influence our conscious decisions and actions; they have an effect, at a conscious level, on the way we behave.

And yet there is evidence of another kind of consciousness that has its roots in the non-physical functions of the brain. It is as if we are, for brief moments, contacted by another force that exists outside our three dimensional world. Almost all of us will acknowledge that there is a higher order of intelligence of which we are a part; this will, from time to time, present itself in a felt presence or awareness; by totally surrendering ego we can come closer to this encompassing intelligent, organising, super force.

In order to do this, it seems that we have first to build our ego - to become self-reliant, to believe we have the ability to do all things and that we are not dependent upon others. We need to recognise self-worth and our uniqueness. When we totally experience this we can let it go completely in reaching out to our spiritual being. Our spirituality recognises that we are, at the same time, nothing and yet part of everything.

Right there at the beginning we were there. Not as we now perceive ourselves, but still we were there. We could come from nowhere else. 150 thousand million years ago, the energy that was to become your life force existed. Realising this, you can never ever again explain anything away as good or bad luck.

All the way down the line choices were being made, until that moment when the ovum that was to become you, was activated into life and made the choice to be male or female - to be you.

Of course, none of this happened by chance. Not in the conscious way we now make our choices, but at a different level, choices were being made. *You were meant to be.*

Spirituality and Conscious Awareness

I have referred to these two states on various occasions throughout this book. I believe they become evident in the way we conduct our lives and is what ultimately gives it direction and purpose.

When we take courage, love, sacrifice, and use them *consciously,* we move nearer the Universal Consciousness that encompasses all. There is no need to put acts of *goodness* into words, they become part of our very being. As humans, such acts are the highest way in which we can utilise the energies we are given.

Being more spiritual is a way of tapping your inner resources and this leads to enlightenment - one experiences insight that has nothing to do with mental functions and yet we are able to bring those insights into consciousness and integrate them into our daily lives. It seems that spiritual insight only becomes truly conscious when we put it into action in our lives.

Summary

1. We do have control over what happens in our lives. Luck is not an invisible force about which we can do nothing.
2. Many things we attribute to luck can be controlled or made to happen by us.
3. Luck is often simply a viewpoint.
4. Money and materialistic things are available to you. There is no special law that says only certain people have the right to them.
5. Most of us need to experience materialistic things in order evolve to a higher level of being.
6. It is possible to learn to dream answers to our problems.
7. By developing our awareness another sense emerges that is not dependent on place or time.
8. Learning to tap on to unconscious processes (those that are outside our conscious control) makes more knowledge available to us.

Finally

It is now time for you to return to your list of things you made at the beginning - those things you believed were dependent on luck - and take another look. See just how many you now view differently, and vow, from this moment onward, to take control and to make things happen for you in this wonderful world of which you are an integral part.

Acknowledgements: My thanks, as always, go to Tom Gregory for all his help and guidance. Also my thanks to Simon Grant and Simeon Jebb for reading the script - where would I be without family and friends!